PreK-K

NUMBER DOT-TO-DOT

Written by **Hanna Otero**

Illustrated by **Creston Ely**

This book belongs to

_____

Copyright © 2004 by Spark Publishing

Colorization & Production by Creative Quotient – A Repro India Limited Enterprise

Flash Kids is a trademark of SparkNotes LLC

All rights reserved. No part of this book may be used or reproduced in any manner whatsoever without the written permission of the Publisher.

ISBN-13: 978-1-4114-9895-2
ISBN-10: 1-4114-9895-X

For more information, please visit _www.flashkidsbooks.com_
Please submit changes or report errors to _www.flashkidsbooks.com/errors_

Printed and bound in China

Spark Publishing
120 Fifth Avenue
New York, NY 10011

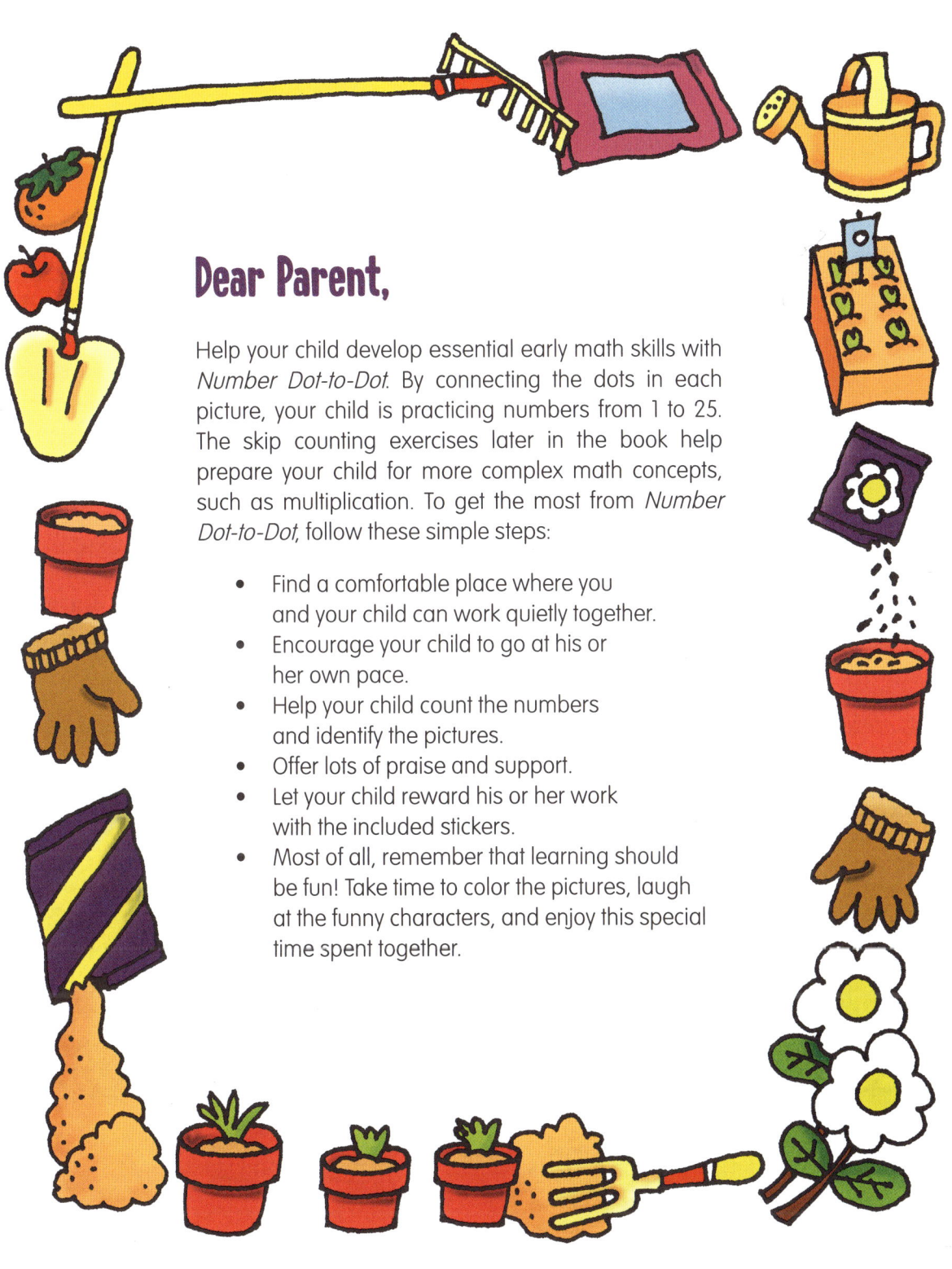

Dear Parent,

Help your child develop essential early math skills with *Number Dot-to-Dot*. By connecting the dots in each picture, your child is practicing numbers from 1 to 25. The skip counting exercises later in the book help prepare your child for more complex math concepts, such as multiplication. To get the most from *Number Dot-to-Dot*, follow these simple steps:

- Find a comfortable place where you and your child can work quietly together.
- Encourage your child to go at his or her own pace.
- Help your child count the numbers and identify the pictures.
- Offer lots of praise and support.
- Let your child reward his or her work with the included stickers.
- Most of all, remember that learning should be fun! Take time to color the pictures, laugh at the funny characters, and enjoy this special time spent together.

It's time to work!

Connect the dots from **1** to **5**.
Color the picture.

Emma wears overalls.

Connect the dots from **1** to **5**.

Color the picture.

We wear boots in the garden.

Connect the dots from **1** to **5**.

Color the picture.

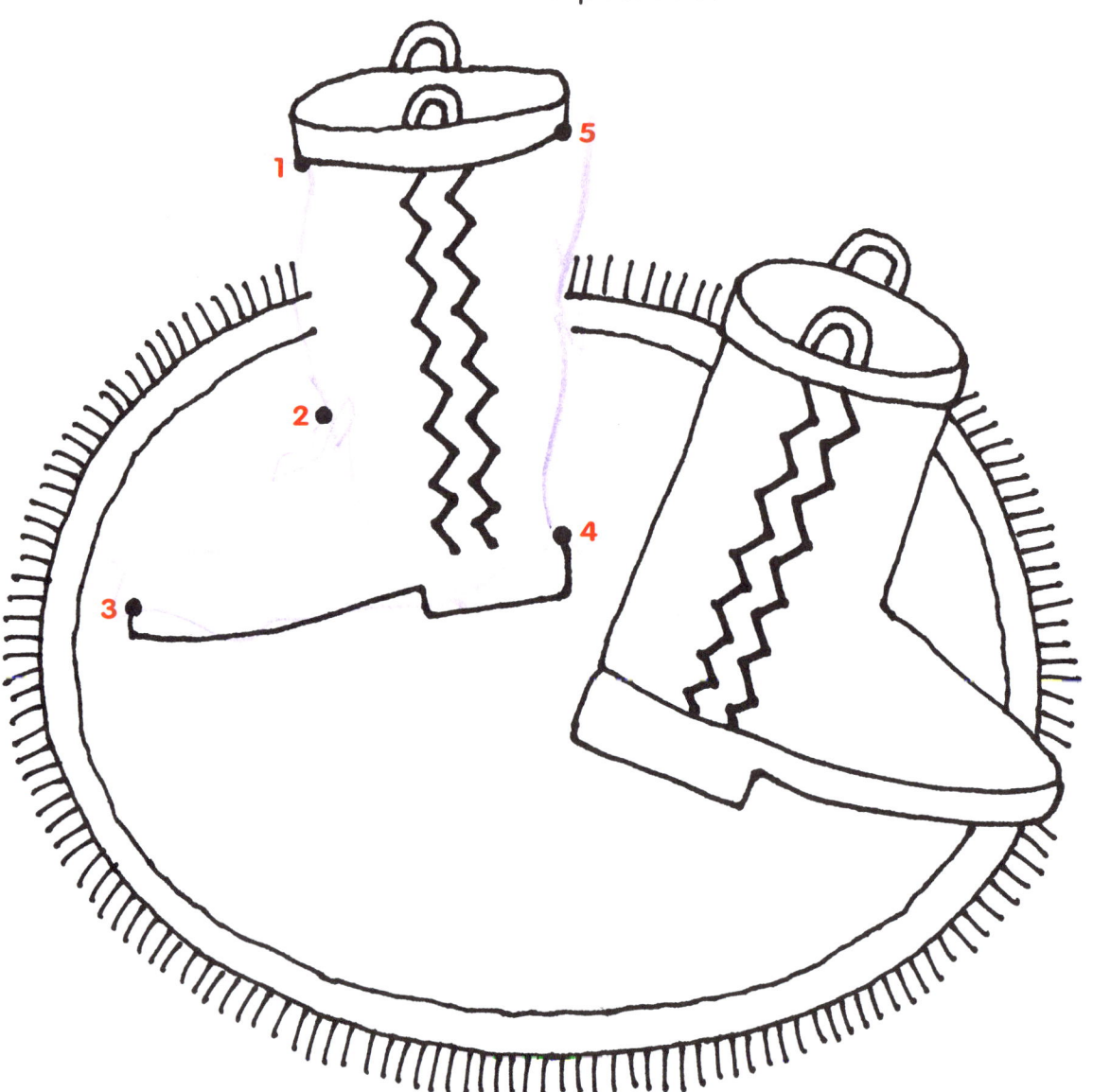

Gloves protect our hands.

Connect the dots from **1** to **5**.

Color the picture.

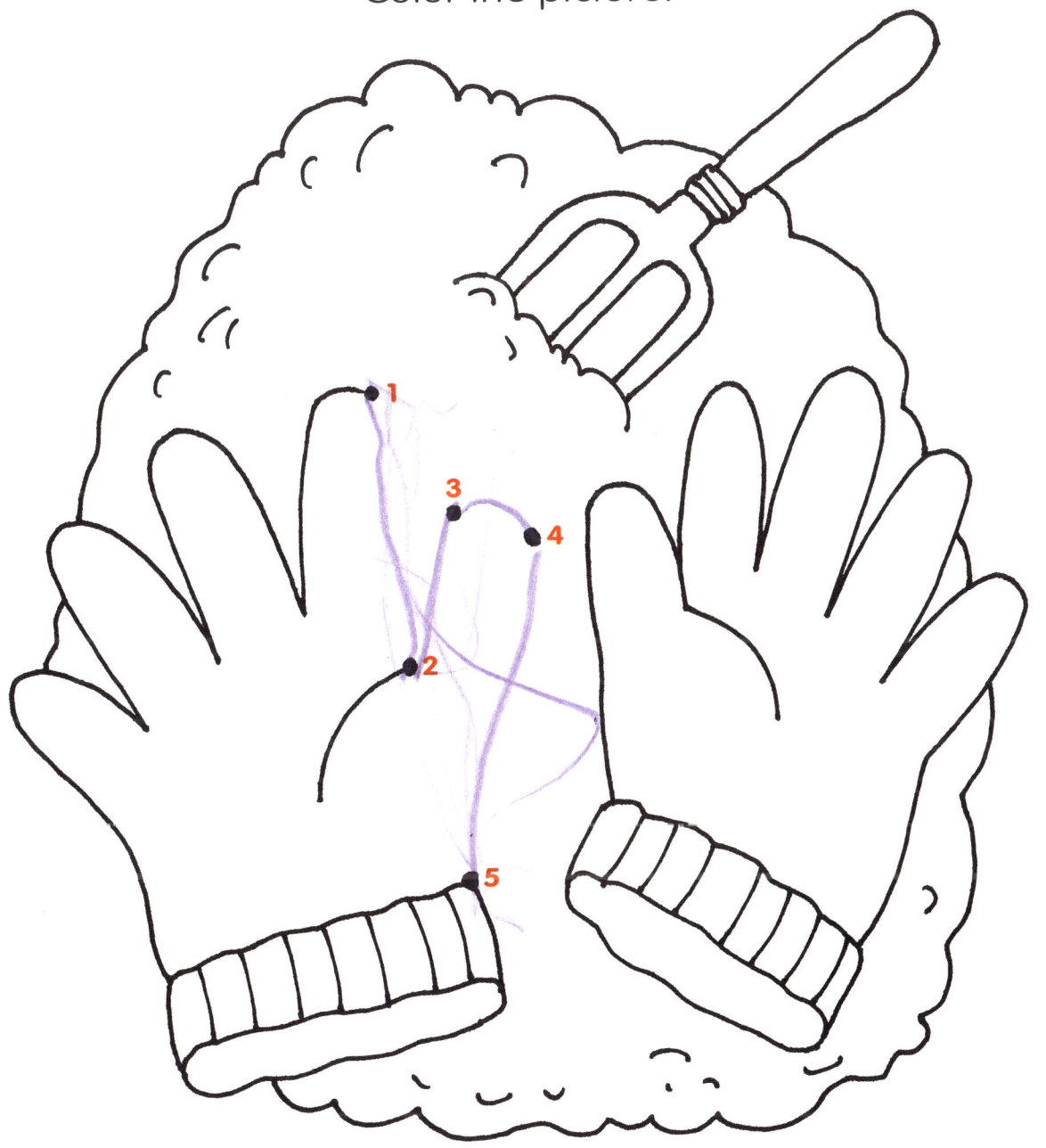

The sun is hot.

Connect the dots from **1** to **5**.
Color the picture.

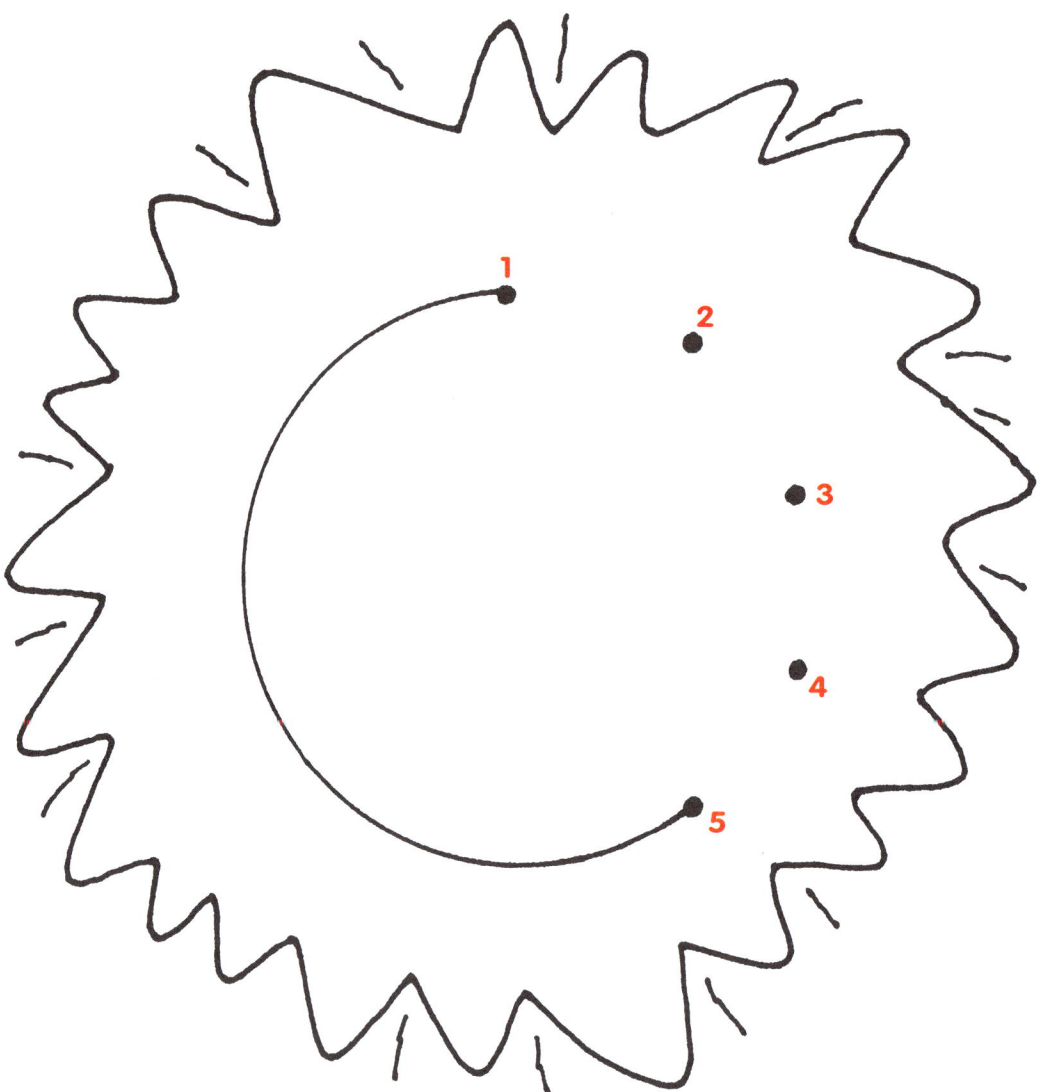

C0-BKW-394

Hats protect our faces.

Connect the dots from **1** to **5**.

Color the picture.

1

2

3

4

5

Rusty works too.

Connect the dots from **1** to **10**.

Color the picture.

We use shovels to dig.

Connect the dots from **1** to **10**.

Color the picture.

We wake a worm.

Connect the dots from **1** to **10**.

Color the picture.

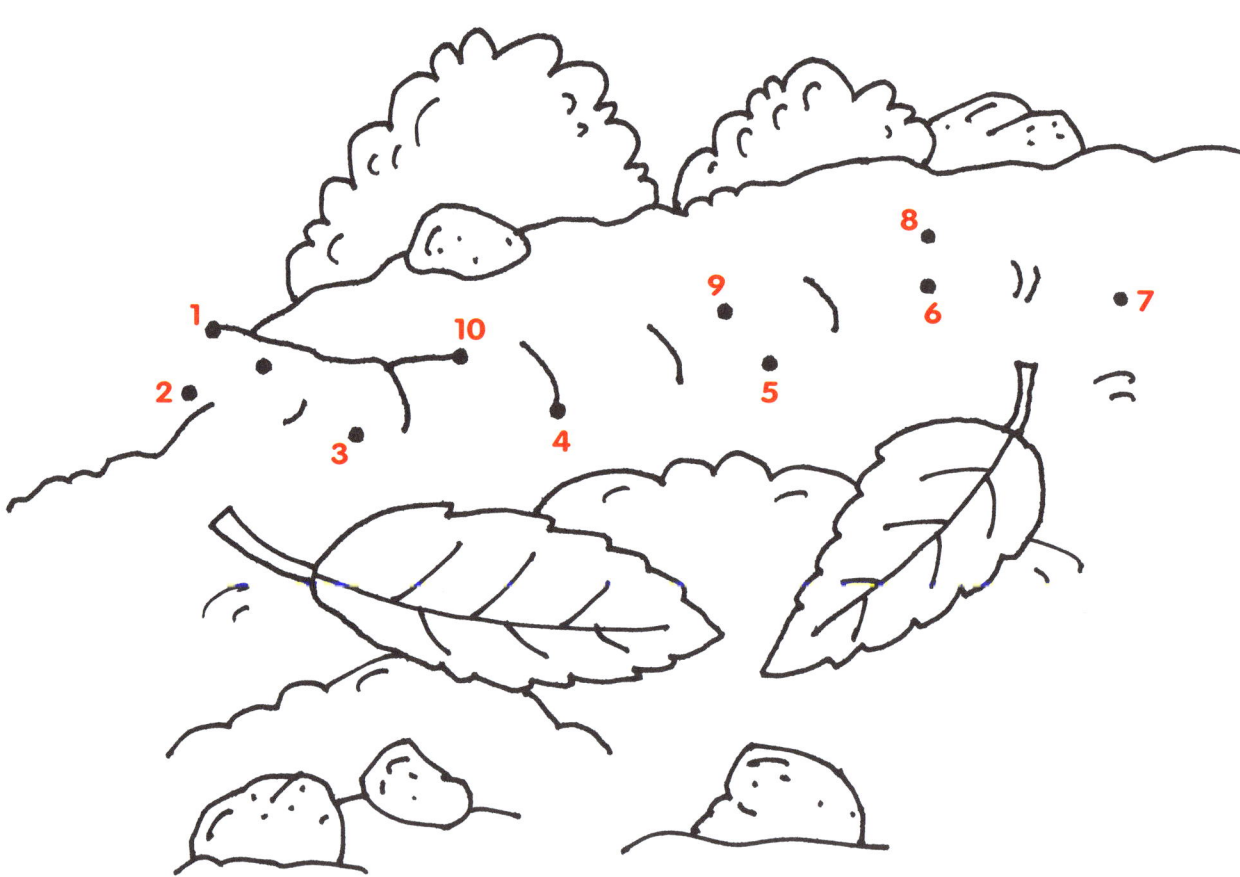

We plant seeds.

Connect the dots from **1** to **10**.

Color the picture.

Soon the seeds will grow.

Connect the dots from **1** to **10**.

Color the picture.

We make a sign.

Connect the dots from **1** to **10**.

Color the picture.

We water the seeds.

Connect the dots from **1** to **10**.
Color the picture.

Many plants grow in our garden.

Connect the dots from **1** to **10**.

Color the picture.

Flowers grow too.

Connect the dots from **1** to **15**.

Color the picture.

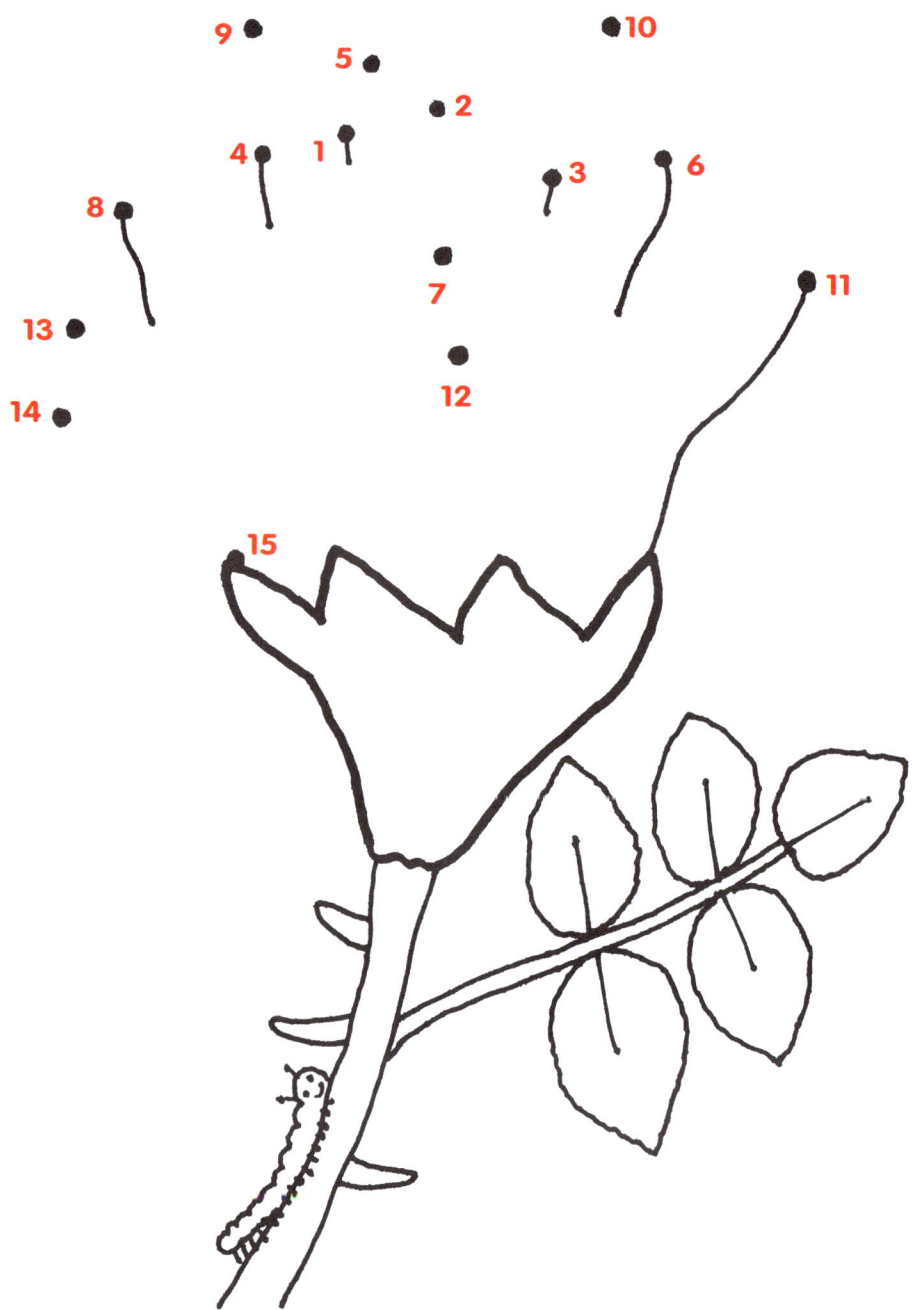

This flower is very tall.

Connect the dots from **1** to **15**.

Color the picture.

Ladybugs like the flowers.

Connect the dots from **1** to **15**.

Color the picture.

Bees like the flowers too.

Connect the dots from **1** to **15**.

Color the picture.

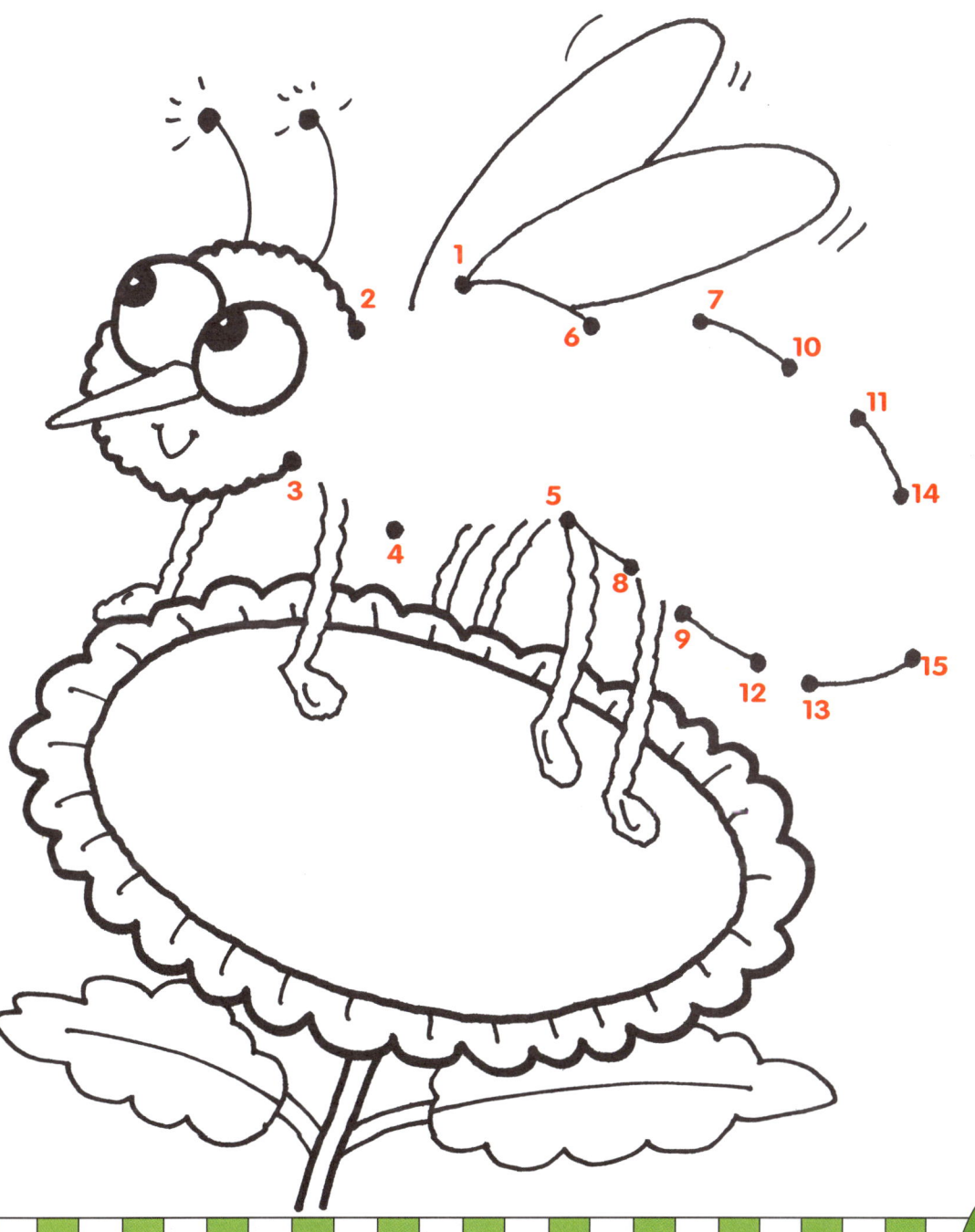

I like the tulips.

Connect the dots from **1** to **20**.
Color the picture.

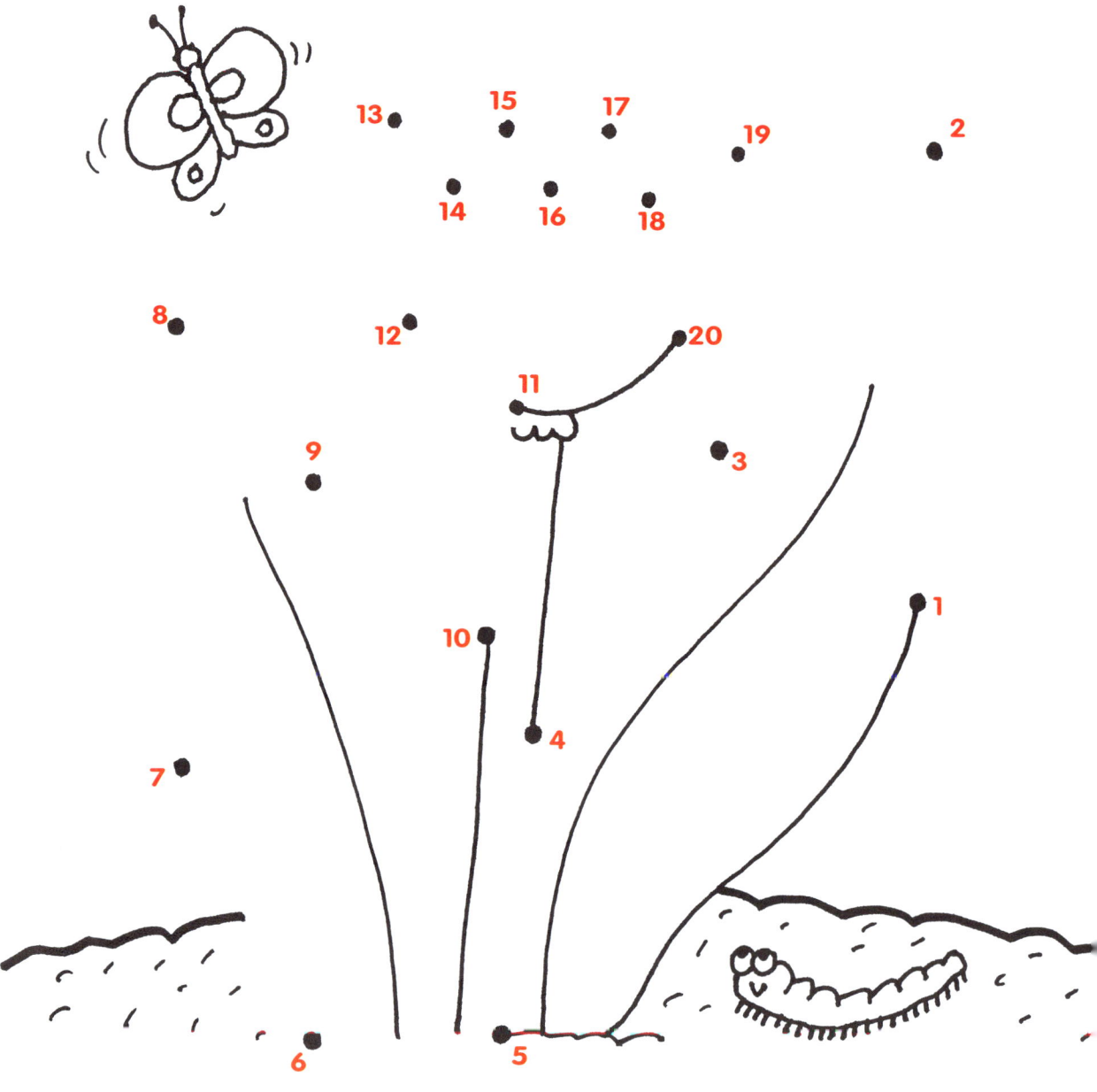

This is Emma's favorite flower.

Connect the dots from **1** to **20**.

Color the picture.

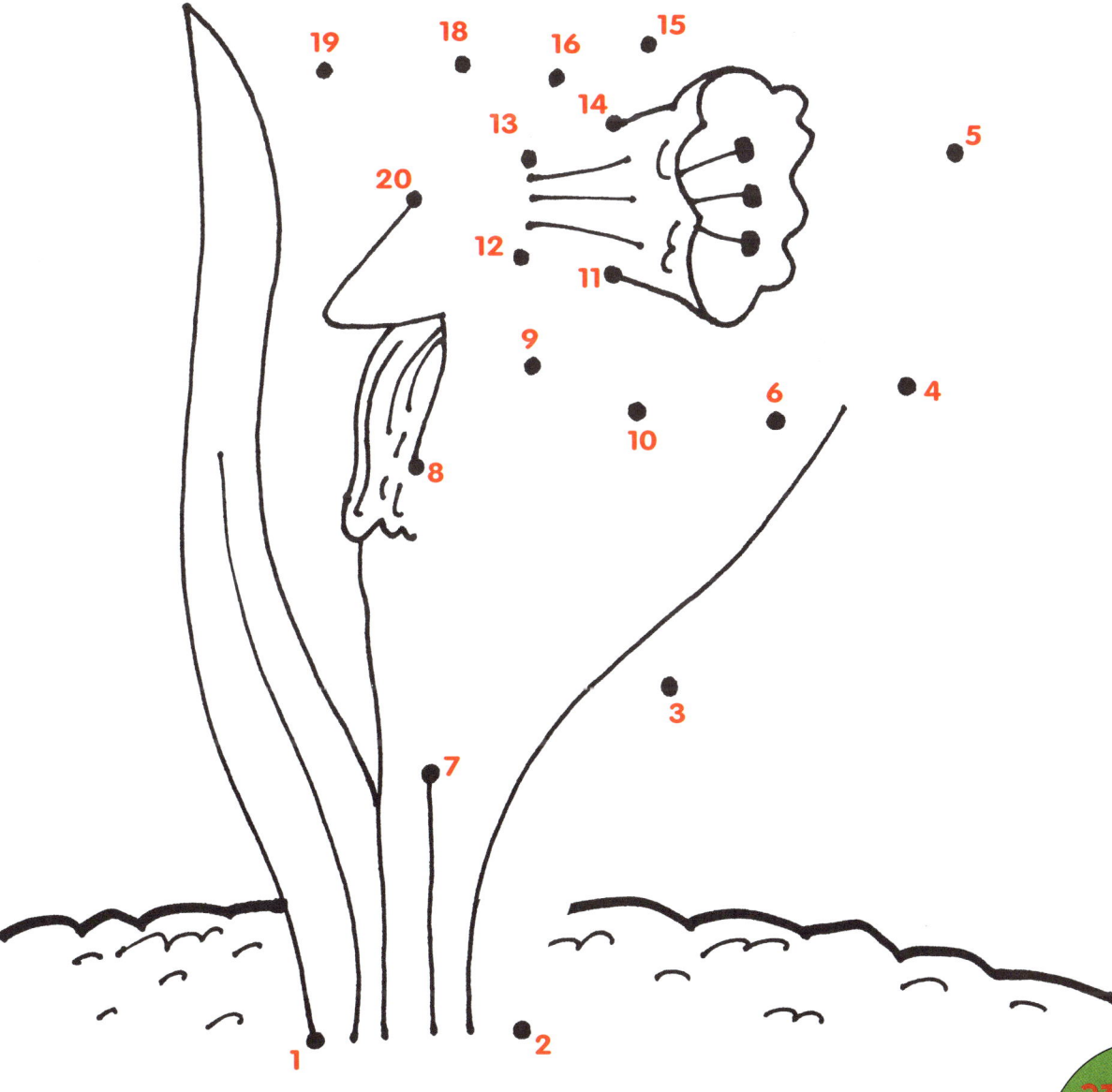

23

A bird watches us work.

Connect the dots from **1** to **20**.

Color the picture.

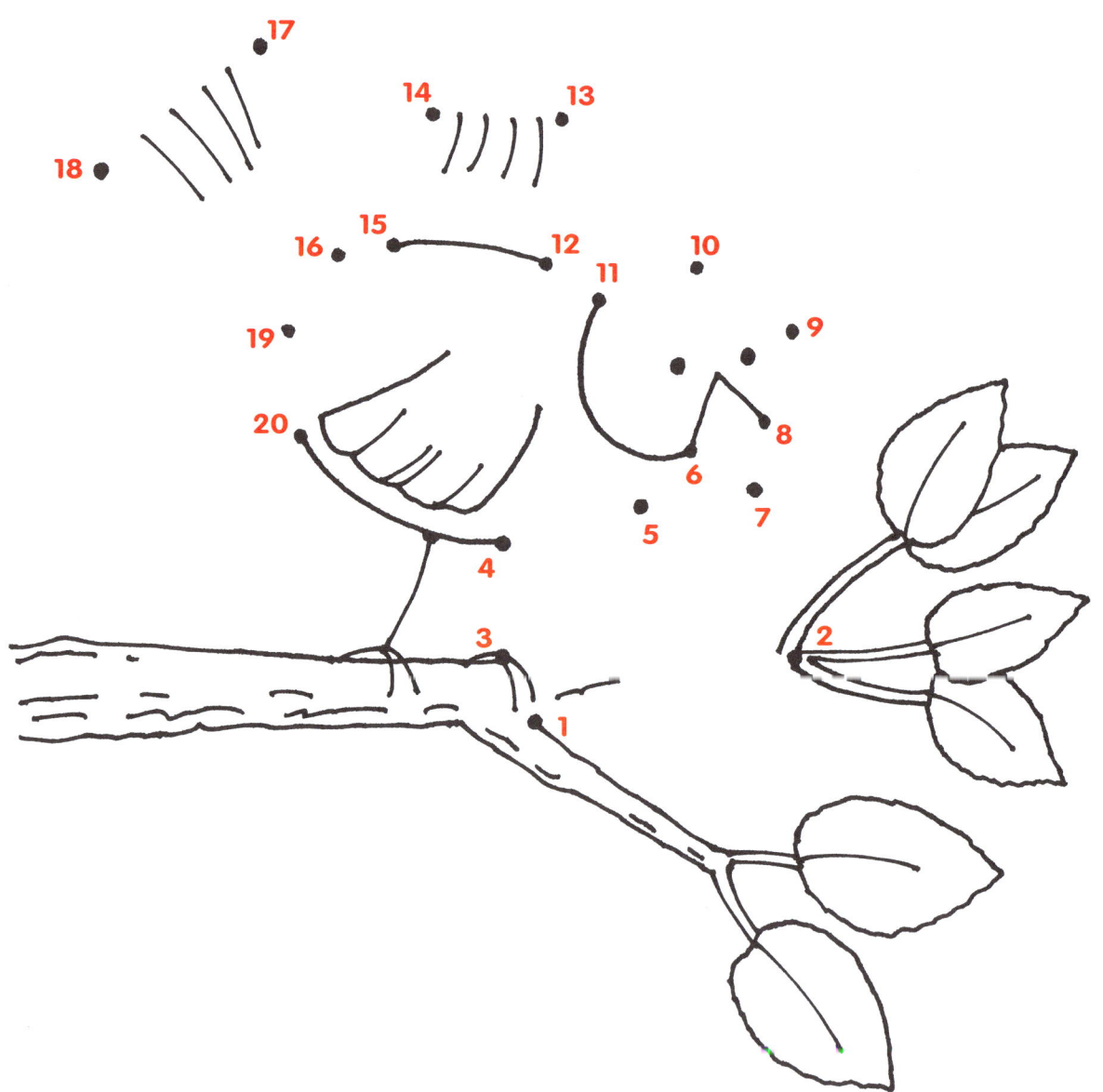

Her babies are nearby.

Connect the dots from **1** to **20**.

Color the picture.

Gus plays in the garden.

Connect the dots from **1** to **20**.

Color the picture.

He sits on the fence.

Connect the dots from **1** to **20**.

Color the picture.

Rusty has a house.

Connect the dots from **1** to **25**.

Color the picture.

The tools are in the shed.

Connect the dots from **1** to **25**.

Color the picture.

A rake is a garden tool.

Connect the dots from **1** to **25**.

Color the picture.

We carry the hose.

Connect the dots from **1** to **25**.

Color the picture.

I help Dad.

Connect the dots from **1** to **25**.
Color the picture.

He picks the lemons.

Connect the dots from **1** to **25**.

Color the picture.

We get a lot of lemons.

Connect the dots. Skip count by twos from **2** to **10**.
Color the picture.

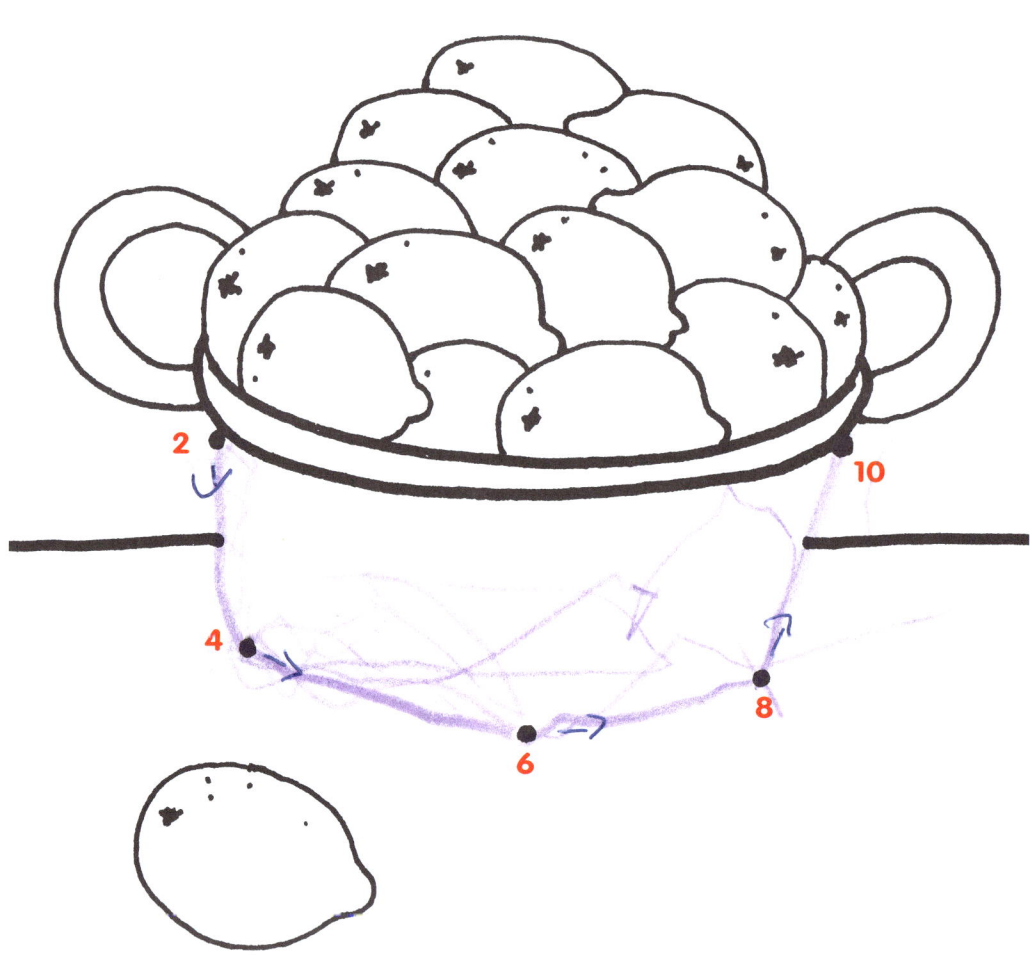

We will make a treat.

Connect the dots. Skip count by twos from **2** to **10**.
Color the picture.

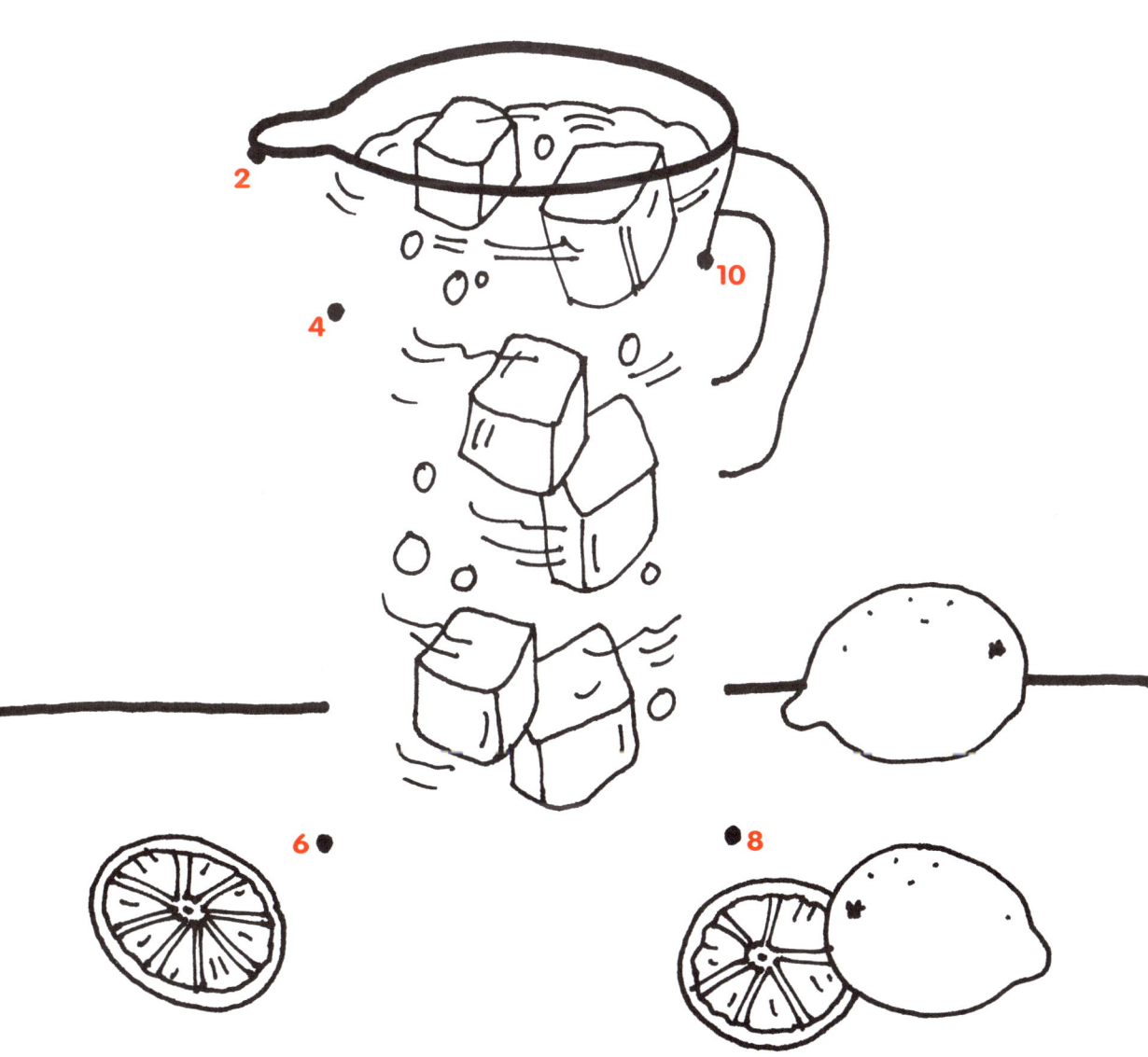

Now we pick vegetables.

Connect the dots. Skip count by twos from **2** to **10**.
Color the picture.

Carrots come from the ground.

Connect the dots. Skip count by twos from **2** to **10**.
Color the picture.

We grow a lot of corn.

Connect the dots. Skip count by twos from **2** to **10**.
Color the picture.

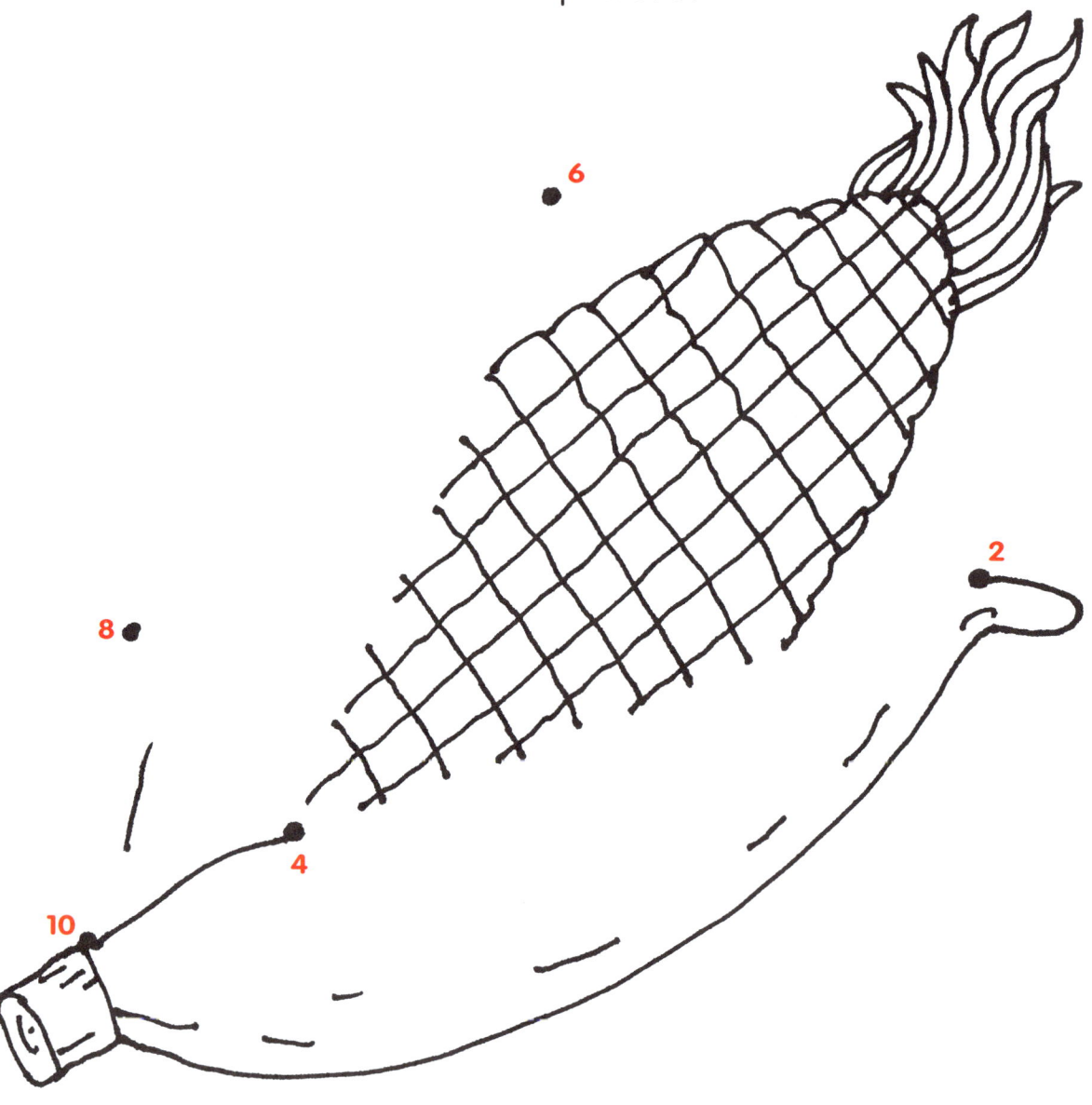

Rabbits eat our vegetables.

Connect the dots. Skip count by twos from **2** to **10**.
Color the picture.

Don't wake the babies!

Connect the dots. Skip count by twos from **2** to **12**.
Color the picture.

We fill the wheelbarrow.

Connect the dots. Skip count by twos from **2** to **12**.
Color the picture.

Time for a break!

Connect the dots. Skip count by twos from **2** to **14**.
Color the picture.

Emma rests her eyes.

Connect the dots. Skip count by twos from **2** to **14**.

Color the picture.

Gus and Rusty rest, too.

Connect the dots. Skip count by twos from **2** to **16**.
Color the picture.

Dad brings the baby.

Connect the dots. Skip count by twos from **2** to **16**.
Color the picture.

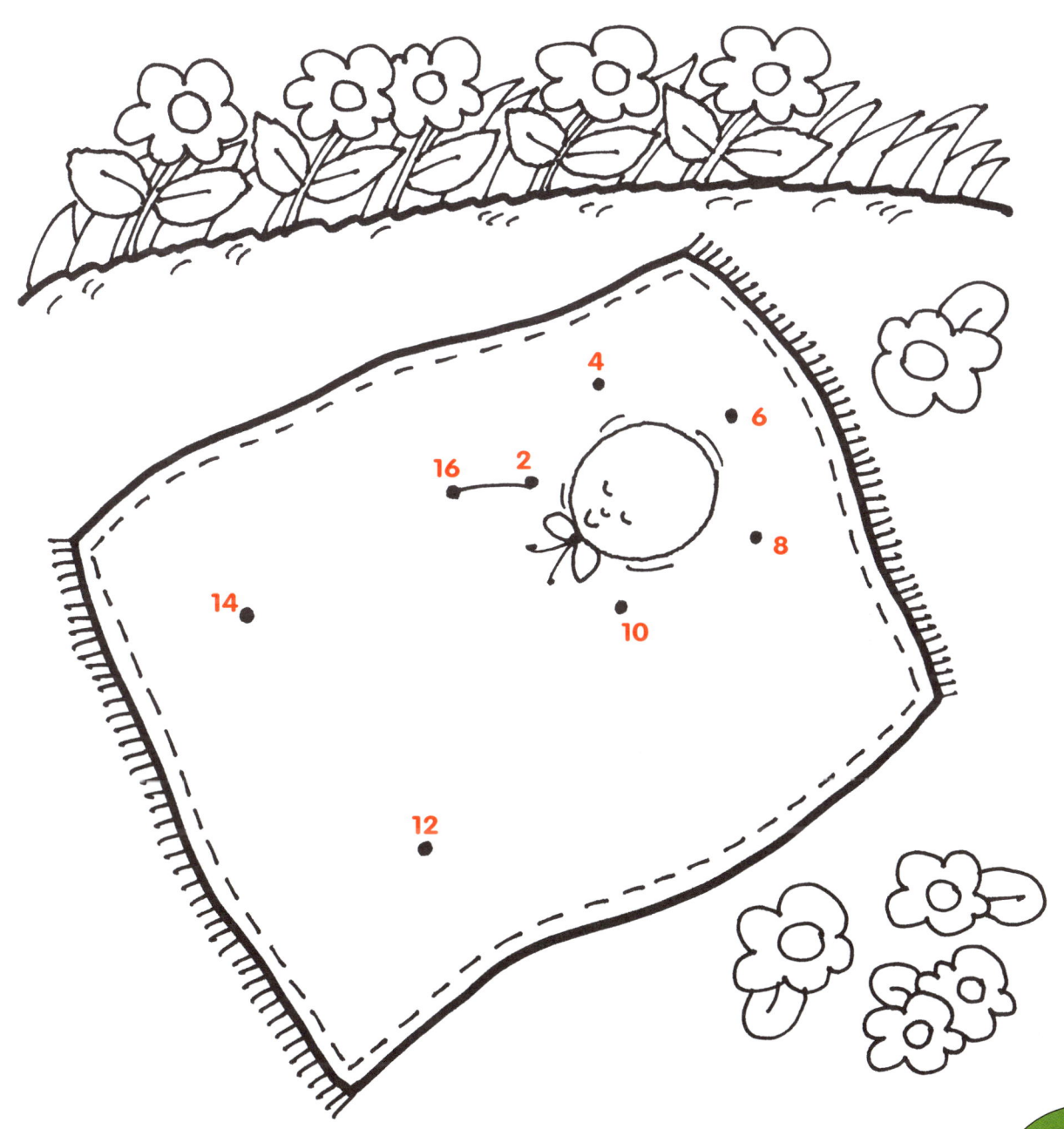

Here is our lunch.

Connect the dots. Skip count by twos from **2** to **16**.
Color the picture.

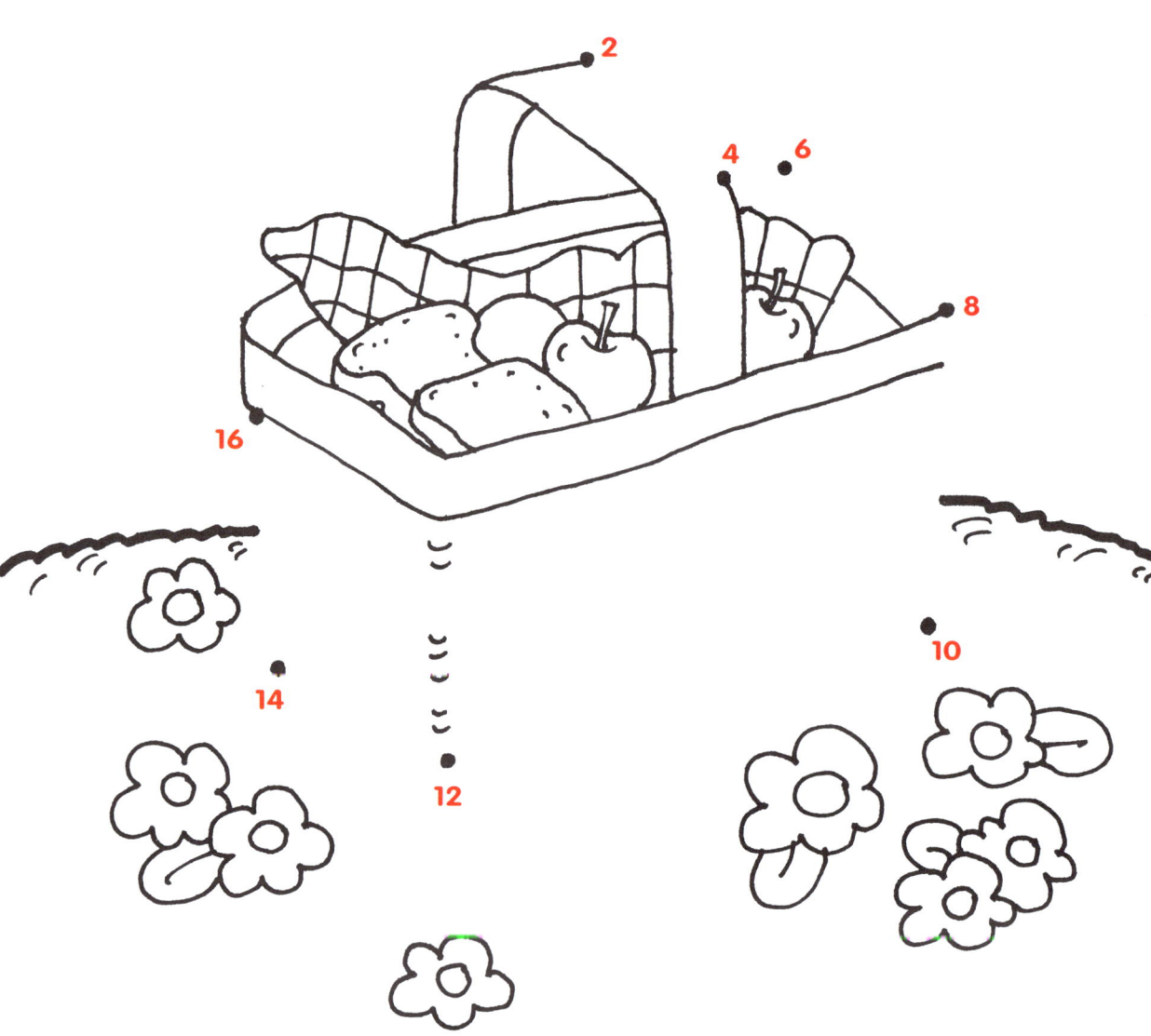

We eat sandwiches.

Connect the dots. Skip count by twos from **2** to **16**.
Color the picture.

We are thirsty!

Connect the dots. Skip count by twos from **2** to **18**.
Color the picture.

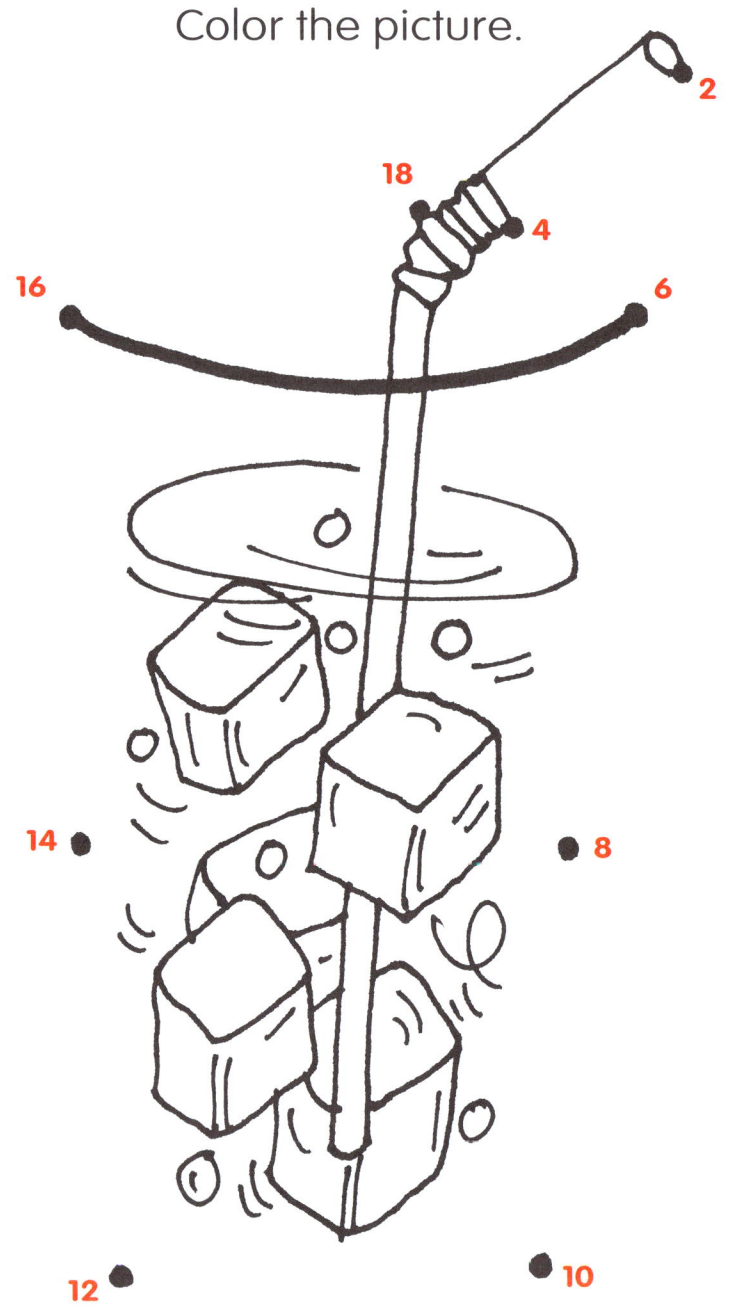

We snack on watermelon.

Connect the dots. Skip count by twos from **2** to **18**.

Color the picture.

A squirrel wants our food.

Connect the dots. Skip count by twos from **2** to **18**.
Color the picture.

Berries are delicious.

Connect the dots. Skip count by twos from **2** to **20**.
Color the picture.

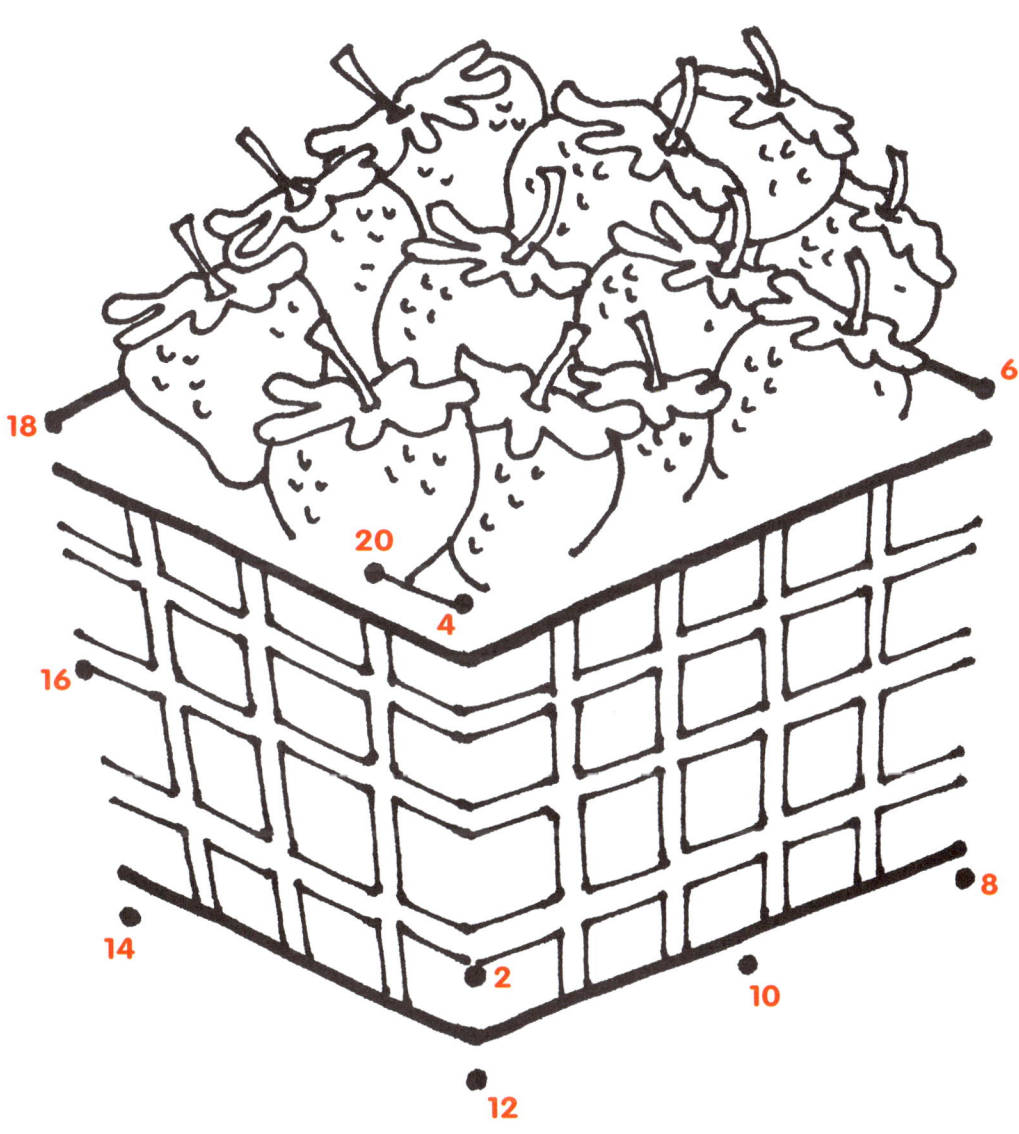

The wind chimes make a nice noise.

Connect the dots. Skip count by twos from **2** to **20**.
Color the picture.

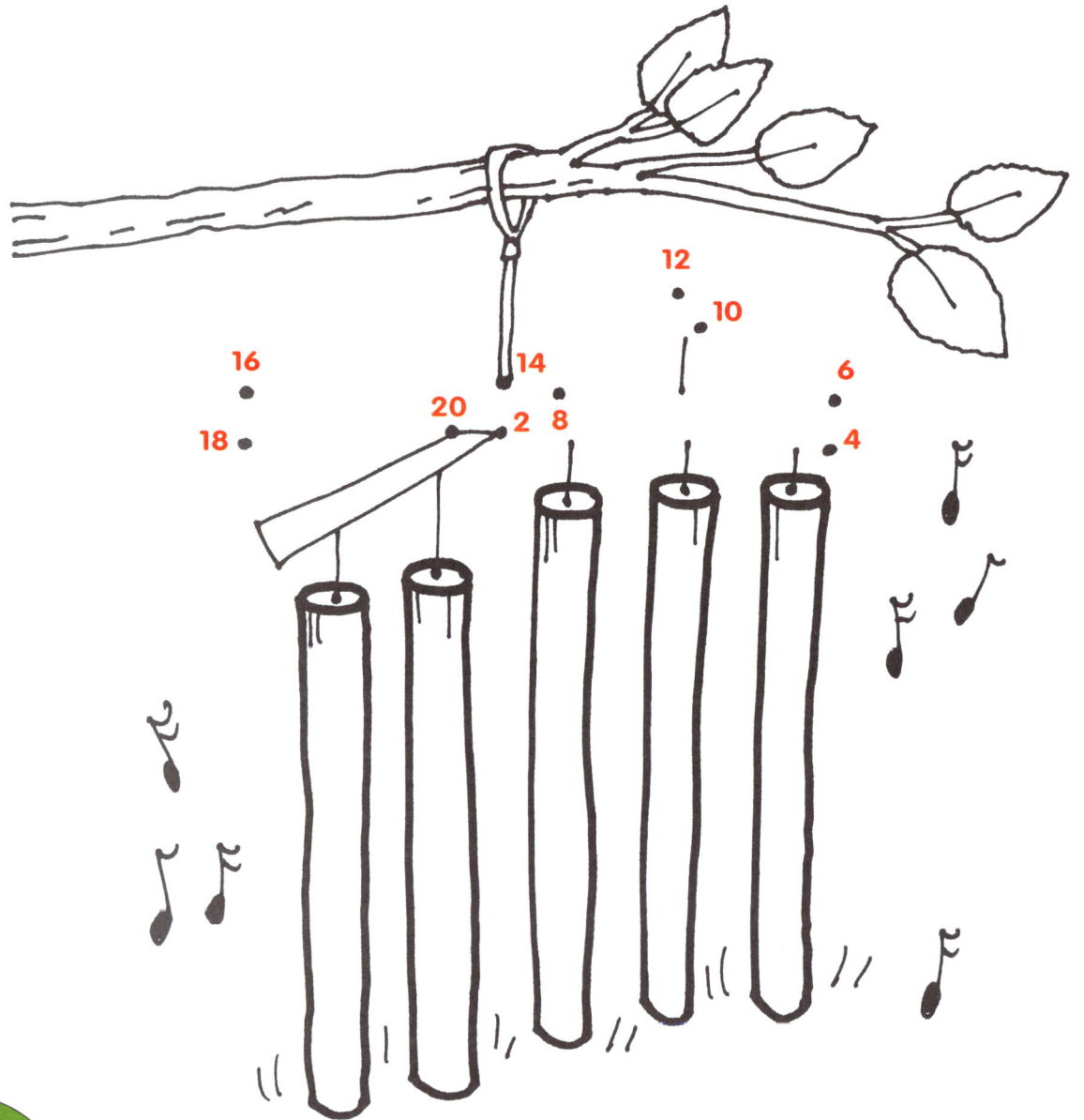

Mom plays some music.

Connect the dots. Skip count by twos from **2** to **20**.
Color the picture.

We take Lily for a ride.

Connect the dots. Skip count by twos from **2** to **20**.
Color the picture.

Our picnic has visitors.

Connect the dots. Skip count by twos from **2** to **20**.
Color the picture.

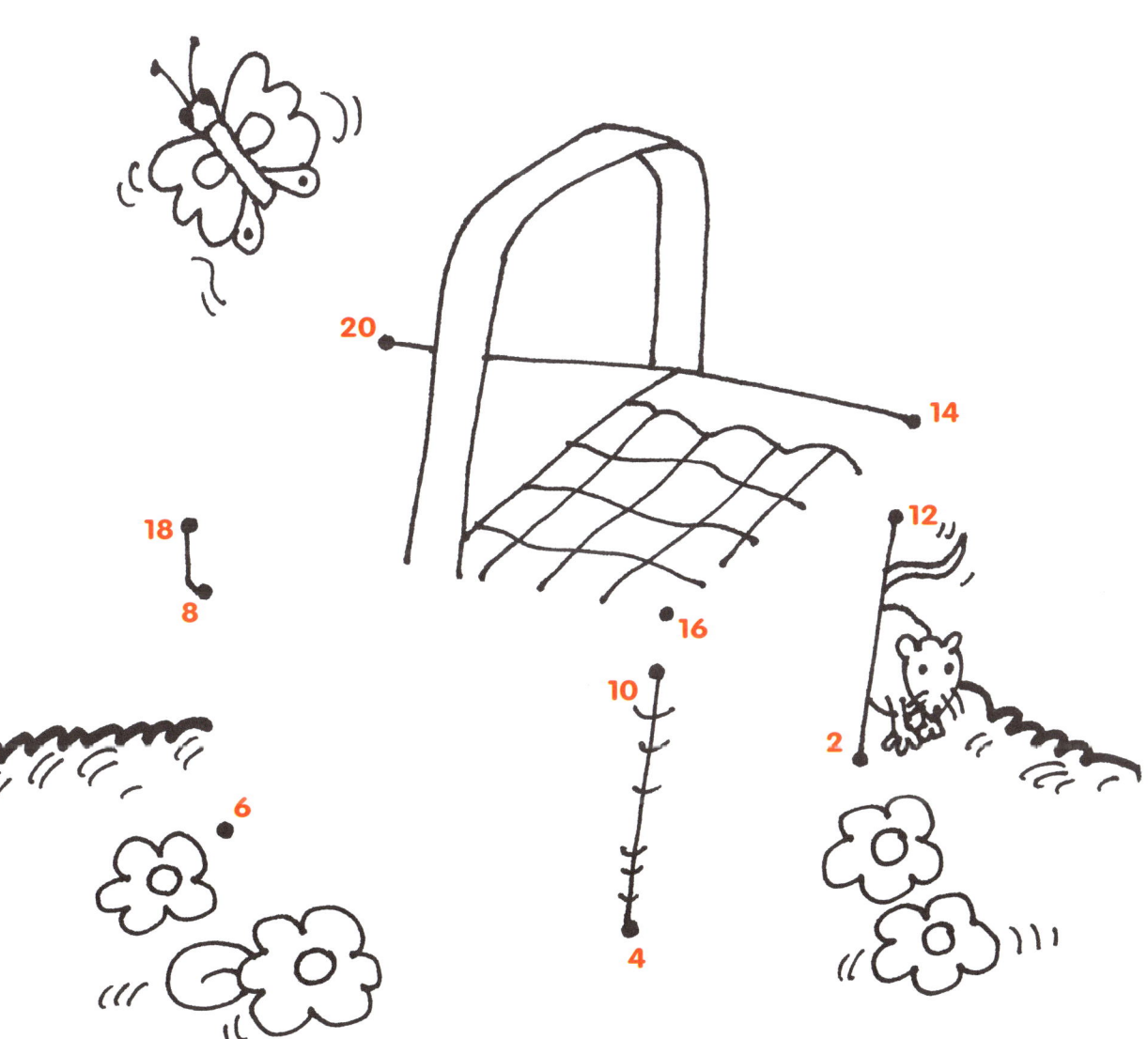

Back to work!

Connect the dots. Skip count by twos from **2** to **20**.
Color the picture.

We make a rock garden.

Connect the dots. Skip count by fives from **5** to **20**.
Color the picture.

We see a little snake.

Connect the dots. Skip count by fives from **5** to **20**.
Color the picture.

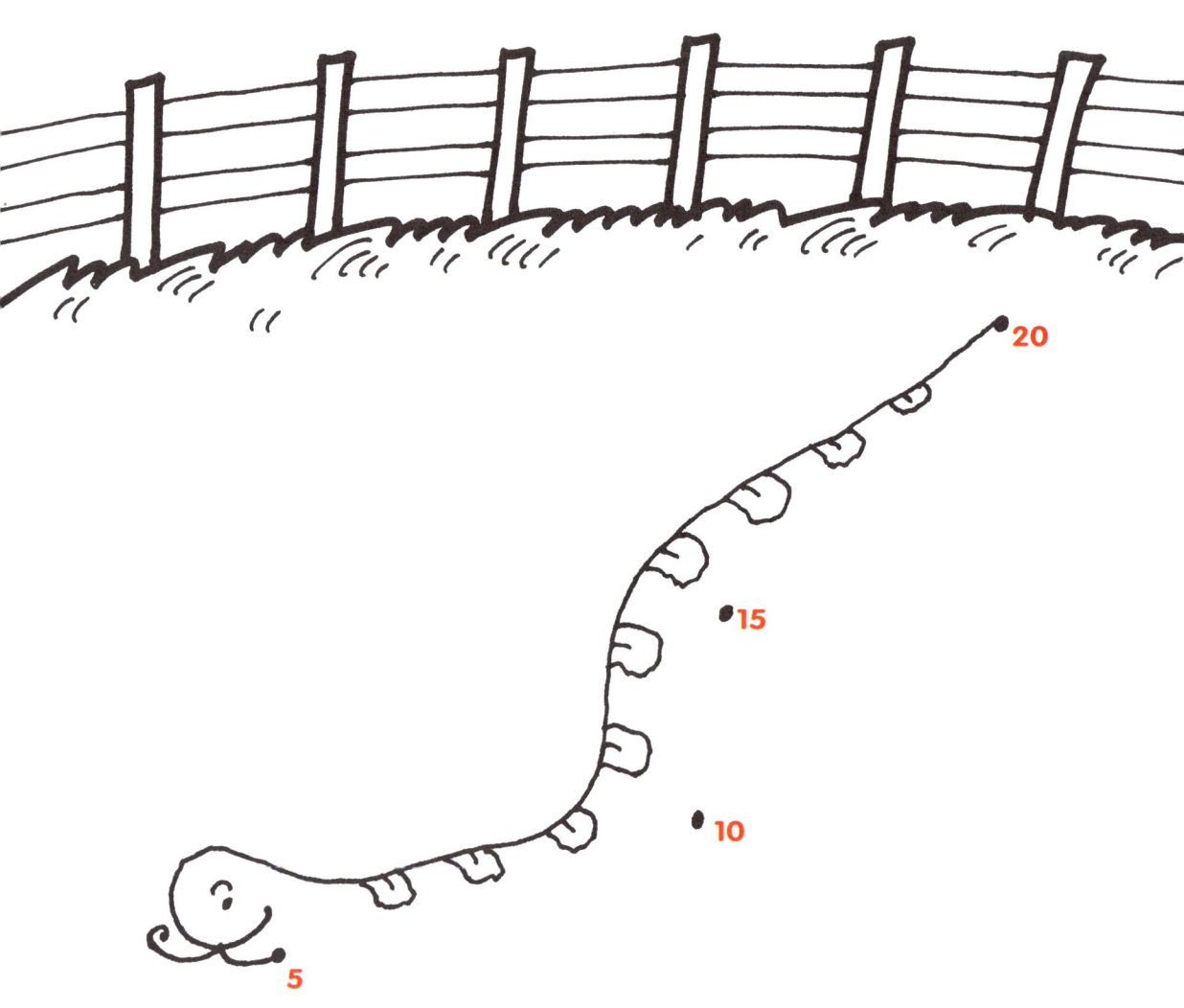

Many creatures live in the grass.

Connect the dots. Skip count by fives from **5** to **25**.

Color the picture.

Butterflies live in the garden too.

Connect the dots. Skip count by fives from **5** to **25**.
Color the picture.

The work is nearly done.

Connect the dots. Skip count by fives from **5** to **25**.
Color the picture.

The sun is setting.

Connect the dots. Skip count by fives from **5** to **25**.
Color the picture.

10

15

20

5

25

Our garden is beautiful.

Connect the dots. Skip count by fives from **5** to **25**.
Color the picture.

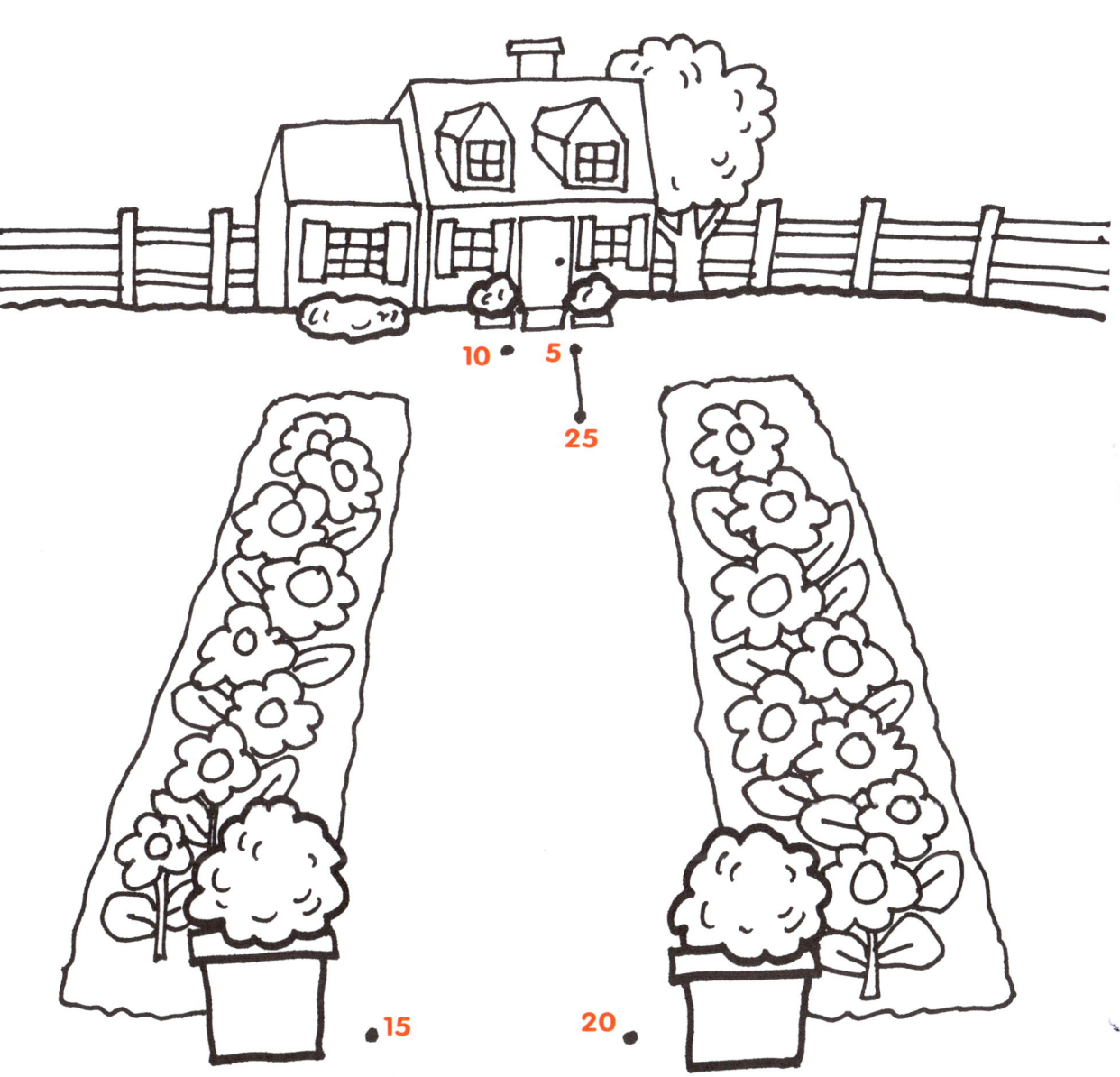

Nice Work!

Congratulations,

_____
(Name)

You connected the dots and finished the story.

It was as easy as 1,2,3!